# HOW SHOULD MEN LEAD
# **THEIR FAMILIES?**

JOEL R. BEEKE

**REFORMATION HERITAGE BOOKS**
GRAND RAPIDS, MICHIGAN

**Reformation Heritage Books**
2965 Leonard St. NE
Grand Rapids, MI 49525
616-977-0889 / Fax 616-285-3246
orders@heritagebooks.org
www.heritagebooks.org

*Printed in the United States of America*
17 18 19 20 21 22/11 10 9 8 7 6 5 4 3

ISBN 978-1-60178-365-3

*For additional Reformed literature, request a free book list from Reformation Heritage Books at the above regular or e-mail address.*

# HOW SHOULD MEN LEAD
## THEIR FAMILIES?

John Paton (1824–1907) was a notable Presbyterian missionary to people in the islands of the South Pacific. Though he was threatened with death, he preached faithfully to cannibals and was used by God for the conversion of many heathen as well as to influence many other godly men to become missionaries. He faced enormous difficulties and sorrows but persevered in the name of Christ. One way God prepared Paton for his work was through his father's example.

Paton's father, James, worked in a shop in the family home in Scotland. James used a small room in the house as a prayer closet, and his regular visits to it deeply affected his son. John said, "Thither daily, and oftentimes a day, generally after each meal, we saw our father retire, and 'shut the door'; and we children got to understand…that prayers were being poured out there for us, as of old by the High Priest within the veil in the Most High Place." The Paton children often sensed their father's fervency in pleading for them before the throne of grace.

When John Paton left his home to study theology in Glasgow, he had to walk forty miles to a train station. His father walked the first six miles with him. They spoke about the Lord, and his father gave counsel. For the last half mile, they walked in silence, but James's lips moved in silent prayer for his son while tears streamed down his face. When they parted, the father grasped his son, saying, "God bless you, my son! May your father's God prosper you and keep you from all evil." Overcome, he could say no more, but his lips continued to move in prayer. Paton later wrote that as he walked the remainder of the distance, he "vowed deeply and oft, by the help of God, to live and act so as never to grieve or dishonor such a father and mother as He had given [him]."[1]

Oh to be a father like James Paton! Christian fathers long to impart spiritual good to their children, but how can we do that when we are so foolish, so weak, and so corrupt in our own sins? We can do it only by walking in the anointing of Jesus Christ.

## OFFICE BEARERS BY UNION WITH CHRIST

The Heidelberg Catechism (Q. 31) says Jesus is called the Christ because Christ means "anointed," and He was ordained by God and anointed by the Spirit for

---

1. John G. Paton, *Missionary to the New Hebrides* (1889; repr., Edinburgh: Banner of Truth Trust, 1994), 8, 25–26. Thanks to Paul Smalley for his assistance in finalizing this article, which is slightly expanded from an address I gave at the Church of the Carolinas, Greenville, South Carolina, on November 20, 2010.

His work as our prophet, priest, and king. What is perhaps more startling is the way the Catechism applies this to us in Christ. After asking, "But why art thou called a Christian?" (Q. 32), the Catechism answers,

> Because I am a member of Christ by faith, and thus am partaker of His anointing; that so I may confess His name [that is our prophetic anointing]; and present myself a living sacrifice of thankfulness to Him [that is our priestly anointing]; and also that with a free and good conscience I may fight against sin and Satan in this life, and afterwards reign with Him eternally, over all creatures [that is our kingly anointing].[2]

Jesus is our mediator. He is our prophet to teach us; our priest to sacrifice, intercede, and bless us; and our king to rule and guide us. In union with Him, we share His offices in a limited but important way. If Christ is not yet your living head, I beg you to be reconciled to God by trusting in Christ alone to save you. You who are in Christ, from the least to the greatest, are all office bearers by union with Christ.

This office-bearing has huge implications for leading our families. As God's ordained representatives to our wives and children, we should serve them as prophets, priests, and kings. The word *father*

---

2. "The Heidelberg Catechism," in *Doctrinal Standards, Liturgy, and Church Order,* ed. Joel R. Beeke (Grand Rapids: Reformation Heritage Books, 1999), 40. Further references from the Heidelberg Catechism are drawn from this translation.

implies that we should be images of the Father of glory, whose brilliance shines fully in His Son. Similarly, if you bear the title *husband*, God calls you to bear the image of our heavenly Husband who loved His bride, the church, and laid down His life to make her holy. We are to reflect all three aspects of Christ's office-bearing to our family in our homes. Let us consider those roles to see how each relates to a man's domestic life.

## PROPHET IN THE HOME

After the Heidelberg Catechism asks why Jesus is called the Christ, or "anointed" (Q. 31), the answer begins, "Because He is ordained of God the Father, and anointed with the Holy Ghost, to be our chief Prophet and Teacher, who has fully revealed to us the secret counsel and will of God concerning our redemption."

Many people think that a prophet is someone who predicts the future. Some prophets predicted future events, such as the coming of Christ, but that was not their central role. The essential task of the prophet is to be God's spokesman to people. The Spirit inspired the prophets and apostles to speak and write God's Word. God's Son is the ultimate, omniscient prophet. As a prophet to your family, you confess your own faith and speak forth the counsel of God given in the Bible. You do not add to the Bible; your task is to make its truths known to your children. This is your prophetic task as a father.

The question we must address is, *How* should you teach as God's prophet in the home? Let me give six guidelines.

1. *Teach with passion.* We have all heard preachers proclaim God's Word in a rather cold, mechanical voice. What a contrast to the prophet Jeremiah's zeal: "His word was in mine heart as a burning fire shut up in my bones, and I was weary with forbearing, and I could not stay" (Jer. 20:9). The prophet tried to hold his peace, but he could not keep God's Word in. He had to speak it forth.

Likewise, Amos, a simple farmer, felt compelled to speak when God called him to do so. He said, "The lion hath roared.... The Lord GOD hath spoken, who can but prophesy?" (Amos 3:8). Many times my dad wept as he taught us the truths of God. That was passionate teaching. My father was bringing us the word of God not as dry, boring information, but as living, "powerful, and sharper than any two-edged sword" (Heb. 4:12). Likewise, we must teach our children with passion.

2. *Teach as God's authorized steward.* Part of our earnestness in speaking to our children comes from knowing that God has appointed us to teach them. Ephesians 6:4 says, "Fathers, provoke not your children to wrath: but bring them up in the nurture and admonition of the Lord." Our children need to understand that God commands us to teach them.

We can say to them, "Children, God gave me this task of teaching you. I must follow His commands." Churches and Christian schools may supplement our efforts, but the primary responsibility of teaching covenant children belongs to parents, especially the father. You cannot delegate all the responsibility to other teachers and consider the job done.

3. *Teach through family worship.* Daily family worship ought to be the foundation of your fatherly exercising of your prophetical office toward your children. Be determined over a period of two decades of family worship to teach your children the whole counsel of God, as Paul said he did for the Ephesians (Acts 20:17–27). Your home is to be a little church, a little seminary, in which you are to serve as an instructing prophet, teaching your children God's precious truth—addressing the mind, the conscience, the heart, and the will of each of your children. Teach your children Bible stories and Bible doctrines, and apply those stories and doctrines to their daily lives, with the Spirit's blessing, for their proper spiritual, moral, and psychological development.

Major on the basics. Teach your children about each Bible book, showing them each book's major theme and how each book leads us as needy sinners to Jesus Christ. Teach them to memorize the Ten Commandments, the Lord's Prayer, and the Apostles' Creed to prepare them for further instruction. Teach them who God is and what He is like. Teach them the origin, comprehensiveness, and seriousness of sin. Teach them the necessity of the new birth and of personal repentance and faith in Christ alone for salvation. Teach them about the atoning blood of Christ and its efficacious power. Present the whole Christ to your children—tell them about His person and natures, His offices and states, and His beauty and all-sufficiency. Teach them about the moral law and its civil, evangelical, and didactic uses. Teach them about God's call to holiness and obedience, and how to live a lifestyle of thankfulness. Set before them the reality of death, the solemnity of judgment, the joy of heaven, the dreadfulness of hell, and the eternality of eternity.

As you teach, be plain in meaning and style. Be experiential and relevant in application. Be affectionate in manner, like the father in Proverbs. Reach down into the life of your children by using age-appropriate illustrations and concrete concepts. Simplify sermons you've heard for them. Tether biblical instruction to current events in your family, society, and nation as much as possible.[3]

4. *Teach by example.* In addition to being our chief prophet, Jesus was the living Word (John 1:1, 14). He revealed God not only in His words but also in His

---

3. This point is mostly abridged from *Bringing the Gospel to Covenant Children*, by Joel R. Beeke (Grand Rapids: Reformation Heritage Books, 2010).

life. So did Paul, who wrote to Timothy, his dear son in the Lord, "But thou hast fully known my doctrine, manner of life, purpose, faith, longsuffering, charity, patience, persecutions, afflictions, which came unto me at Antioch, at Iconium, at Lystra; what persecutions I endured: but out of them all the Lord delivered me" (2 Tim. 3:10–11). We are always teaching our children, whether we know it or not, for they are always reading the book of our lives. Besides the Bible, your lives are the most important book your children will ever read. In the book of your life, they will see how important your views on God are, whether worship is a delight or a duty, whether sin is a horrible evil or mere naughtiness, and whether we really cherish our families or view them as a burden.

5. *Teach by sharing your life*. Paul openly spoke about his problems, afflictions, and weaknesses. He boasted in his weaknesses so that others could see the power of Christ in him and the sufficiency of God's grace in all his trials (2 Cor. 12:9–10). He opened his life to others so that they would open their lives to him (2 Cor. 6:11–13). Happy are the children who can say to their friends, "My mom and dad are pretty neat; I can talk to them about anything." That does not mean you act as their buddy—that would negate your authority over them as godly parents. But it does mean we should strive to become their confidants in a friendship that grows as they mature. Jesus called His disciples "friends" because He loved

them enough to die for them and to share with them the whole counsel of God (John 15:13–15).

Moses said in Deuteronomy 6:4–7,

> Hear, O Israel: The LORD our God is one LORD: and thou shalt love the LORD thy God with all thine heart, and with all thy soul, and with all thy might. And these words, which I command thee this day, shall be in thine heart: and thou shalt teach them diligently unto thy children, and shalt talk of them when thou sittest in thine house, and when thou walkest by the way, and when thou liest down, and when thou risest up.

God gave us this great commandment. Jesus also gave the Great Commission to His disciples, commanding them to make disciples throughout the earth, beginning at home. Notice that the context for all of this teaching is life. Consider your prophetic work not just an event in your schedule but an aspect of sharing all of life with your dear ones.

6. *Teach for holistic maturity.* In addition to training their minds, train your children's hearts and souls so they may grow and mature in serving God. Luke 2:52 tells us that "Jesus increased in wisdom and stature, and in favour with God and man." Christ is our model of child development; He was born a baby but grew into an adult in all aspects of His manhood.

Train your children in social graces. A well-trained mind unaccompanied by basic manners or culture is a blunt sword. Our children should show respect to older people, kindness to their peers, and compassion to persons younger than they are. If you expect your children to behave well but have not taught them proper etiquette, you will set them up for failure in society. Furthermore, give them opportunities to enjoy fine art, great literature, and good music as gifts of God's common grace. This too will mature them and enhance their lives.

Train your children physically. Teach your children that their bodies are gifts from God, so they must respect the rules of health and treat their bodies with honor. They need a certain amount of sleep, a healthy diet, and plenty of exercise. Teach your children the facts of life, discussing openly the goodness, spiritual significance, and God-given boundaries of their sexuality. Do not leave that education to their peers. Guide them in matters of personal appearance so that they dress modestly and attractively, but not to draw attention to themselves.

Likewise teach them a balanced view of sports. Recreational sports are a natural part of a child's physical development; children enjoy developing agility and increased strength as they play them. Sports provide much-needed exercise. Participation in sports also teaches them teamwork, leadership, and perseverance. But do not surrender to the sports mania that makes winning everything or allows sports to become a scheduling monster that eats up family time.

Brothers, our prophetic role in the home places great responsibilities upon us. How can we live up to such a calling? Instead of throwing in the towel because of our inadequacies, we should come before God in prayer and say, "I am a sinful human being, but Lord, help me confess my sin, my inconsistent walk, my ignorance of the Bible, and my failure to evangelize my children. Let me be grieved by these failures, turn to Thee for grace to realize my covenantal responsibilities, and take refuge in Thee, leaning on Thy covenant promises and looking to Jesus Thy Son as my model, my guide, and my strength." In the long run, the faithful prophet-father will marvel at God's grace covering his sins and making his efforts bear fruit far beyond the limits of mere human power and wisdom. God is not setting us up to fail as husbands and fathers. He gives us the marvelous grace of being His assistants in teaching our families.

## PRIEST IN THE HOME

When question 31 of the Heidelberg Catechism asks why Jesus is called the Christ, the second part of its answer is, "to be our only High Priest, who by the one sacrifice of His body, has redeemed us, and makes continual intercession with the Father for us." Christ's priestly work was His loving self-sacrifice for our sins and His compassionate intercession for us (Heb. 5:1–2; 7:23–27).

The Bible says that we who trust in Christ are a royal priesthood, authorized and anointed to perform priestly service in God's spiritual temple (1 Peter 2:5, 9). We can never repeat the once-for-all sacrifice of

Christ for sin because Jesus has finished the work to make His elect people perfect (Heb. 10:12, 14). Nor do we stand as mediators between God and man, for there is one Mediator (1 Tim. 2:5–6). Thus, your children do not need to go to God through you but through Christ, the only way (John 14:6). Yet, because of our union with Christ, we actively share in His priesthood in other ways. The Bible calls redeemed people priests (Rev. 1:6; 5:10; 20:6) who offer sacrifices of praise; good works (Heb. 13:15–16); and "supplications, prayers, [and] intercessions…for all men" (1 Tim. 2:1). Let us look at two ways in which a man should operate as a priest in his home.

1. *Sacrifice yourself for your wife.* Paul says in Ephesians 5:25–26, "Husbands, love your wives, even as Christ also loved the church, and gave himself for it; that he might sanctify and cleanse it with the washing of water by the word." William Gouge wrote in 1622 that all the duties of a husband are comprised under this one word: *love*.[4] When we love with a Christlike love, we serve as spiritual priests who offer a pleasing sacrifice to the Lord. We know this is true because Paul wrote in Ephesians 5:2, "Walk in love, as Christ also hath loved us, and hath given himself for us an offering and a sacrifice to God for a sweet-smelling savour."

---

4. William Gouge, *Domestical Duties* (Edinburgh, Ind.: Puritan Reprints, 2006), 251.

What does it mean to love your wife like a priest? It means loving your wife as Christ loved the church (Eph. 5:25). The church is a particular group of people whom God chose before time began and called to salvation. Though the Lord loves all people and commands them to turn back to Him (Acts 17:25, 30), He has a particular and exclusive love for His elect (Rom. 1:7; Gal. 2:20; Eph. 2:4–5; 1 Thess. 1:4). So men must love their wives with a particular and exclusive love in which no other woman may share. Reserve that love as a seal on your heart. With this love, you are not just avoiding adultery; you are intentionally pouring out your affections upon your wife in rich and regular ways. Say to her, "You have ravished my heart" (Song 4:9). Set her "as a seal upon thine heart" (Song 8:6). You may not realize how important it is for your wife to know that you have forsaken all others to love her alone until death separates you, but it is. Neither can you estimate the security and happiness your children receive as they see you love their mother with an exclusive, binding love.

Love your wife, too, with a self-giving love. Again, Ephesians 5:25 explains that "Christ…loved the church, and gave himself for it." Jesus voluntarily died as the surety, substitute, and representative of His elect people. He stood under the curse of God for our sins. In giving Himself, Christ gave His most precious treasure, for He was of infinite value. He was crucified on the cross for unworthy, ungrateful enemies of God.

So, brother, love your wife with self-giving love. Sacrifice for her. Provide for her and cherish her just as you love your own body. Give her your thoughts, your time, your talk, your tenderness, and your touch—but make sure you touch her heart before you touch her body. Stop measuring out your love in small spoonfuls according to what she has done for you lately. Start pouring out your love by the bucket according to the infinite riches of Christ's love for you.

Also, love your wife with a sanctifying love. Christ gave Himself for His bride "that he might sanctify and cleanse it with the washing of water by the word." His sacrifice aimed at purifying our lives from sin so that we would be holy for Him. He applies His sacrifice to us in the living water of the Holy Spirit and the living truth of the Word. Paul viewed his gospel ministry as a priestly work of presenting the nations holy to the Lord, sanctified by the Holy Spirit (Rom. 15:16). In the same way, love your wives with the priestly goal of making them holy to the Lord.

The most important gift you can give your wife is not money, a house, a car, jewelry, or even yourself. The best gift you can give her is to bring her to God so that she can glorify Him and enjoy Him forever. So speak the Word of God to her. Pray for her soul, both in your private prayer times and with her.

Do not make her feel like she has to badger you into being a spiritual leader. Put your heart into leading your family to Christ. Invest your time in her spiritual growth. Sacrifice yourself so that she will have time to read the Word and participate in Bible study or women's conferences.

Brothers, God calls you to a priestly ministry with your wives. While you cannot be her savior, you can be a flesh-and-blood image of the Savior. God loves our wives so much. It is astonishing that He would give poor, weak, foolish, and corrupt men such as we are an influence over them. But in Christ, our priest, we have everything we need to serve our wives in a priestly manner.

2. *Intercede for your children.* A significant part of Christ's work as our Great High Priest is His intercession for us at God's right hand. It is an important part of the teaching of the book of Hebrews (2:18; 4:14–16; 6:20; 7:24–8:2; 9:12, 24; 10:21; 12:2). Christ's intercession is effective to save us to the uttermost. Our prayers cannot compare to His, but Christian fathers can and do share in Christ's priestly work by praying for their children.

We see this priestly work in the way Job ministered before the Lord for his family. We read in Job 1:1, 4–5:

> There was a man in the land of Uz, whose name was Job; and that man was perfect and upright, and one that feared God, and eschewed evil....

> And his sons went and feasted in their houses, every one his day; and sent and called for their three sisters to eat and to drink with them. And it was so, when the days of their feasting were gone about, that Job sent and sanctified them, and rose up early in the morning, and offered burnt offerings according to the number of them all: for Job said, It may be that my sons have sinned, and cursed God in their hearts.

Like Job, intercede for your children out of reverence and godly fear. Job showed his reverence for God by interceding for his children. If you do not pray for your children, how can you say that you fear the Lord? It should not take some tragedy or moral disaster to make you pray for your family. The more I study this passage, the more I am convinced that it does not say that the children of Job were doing anything ungodly. Apparently they were gathering at each other's homes, each taking a turn in hosting fellowship together, but with little or no concern for their own souls. Their father, knowing the tendency of our hearts to sin in secret thoughts and desires, continued to pray for them. Similarly, we should pray for our children, knowing that we must bring even the secret sins of their hearts to the Holy One. Let us not rest in the mere outward conformity of our children to godliness. Let us pray in the fear of the Lord, knowing that our hearts, and theirs, are deeply corrupt.

Intercede for your children with urgency. We are told that Job offered burnt offerings for his children "early in the morning." Spurgeon says, "He wanted to hurry to the cross every morning with his children." He did not offer those sacrifices before bedtime, thinking, "I'd better say a quick prayer for my kids." No, early in the morning Job committed his children to the Lord. We must do likewise for ourselves and our children. These early morning sacrifices indicate Job's earnestness, constancy, and priorities. Praying was the first and most important thing he did every day. How grateful Job must have been in his later years that he had prayed for his children so faithfully before their lives ended in tragedy! We do not know how much time we or any one of our sons or daughters will remain on this earth. Pray for them.

Intercede for your children with perseverance. The Scripture says, "Thus did Job *continually*." Are you faithful in the priestly work of intercession? I am not asking if you pray enough for your children; no one prays enough. But will you pray *daily* for your children, one by one, that each may know his sin, each may be kept from sin, each may fly to the Savior, and each may live a life of holiness? Have you given up on a particular child? Dear brother, is anything too hard for the Lord? Keep on praying; while there is life, there is hope.

Intercede for your children by faith in Christ. Even though he lived before God gave the law to Israel, Job understood there could be no remission of sin without the shedding of blood. He had to kill a

bullock for each child. This involved a great invest-
ment of time, energy, and money, but Job did so
willingly. He killed an animal, laid it on the altar,
and offered it to the Lord. In doing so, he was declar-
ing his faith in the Holy Sacrifice to come. Today
we do not have to kill animals; we can go directly
to Jesus, who has shed His blood for us once and
for all. Inspired by faith, we turn continually to the
covenant-keeping God, committing our children
to His blood. We serve our families as priests by
looking to the Great High Priest, whose blood and
righteousness can save the most hardhearted child
and drive out the most stubborn sin of a believer.

What an amazing privilege Christ has granted
us, to be priests in Him and unto Him! Let us not
neglect this opportunity. Make your home a holy
temple in which you offer daily sacrifices of love for
your wife. Lift prayers for your children like sweet-
smelling incense to the throne of grace. The more
you exercise your priestly ministry as a husband and
father, the more you will discover the presence of
the living God in your family.

## KING IN THE HOME

The Heidelberg Catechism explains Christ's anointing as king, saying, "He is ordained of God the
Father, and anointed with the Holy Ghost, to be…
our eternal King, who governs us by His word and
Spirit, and who defends and preserves us in (the
enjoyment of) that salvation, He has purchased

for us" (Q. 31). Like David, the most favored king of Israel, Jesus serves as king of His people by ruling over us with justice and destroying our enemies with His might (2 Sam. 8:13–15).

The Son of God is the Most High King, supreme in His authority and sovereign in His power. Christ alone can bind our conscience with sacred obligation and change our hearts. Christ alone can judge, vindicate, and condemn people for eternity. Though dictators, tyrants, and other oppressors pretend godlike majesty, they cannot usurp the Lord's throne. But God graciously extends the sure mercies of His covenant with David (Isa. 55:3) to all believers, granting us the promise to reign with Him as kings (Rev. 1:6; 5:10; 20:4, 6; 22:5). Indeed, it was God's purpose in creation that man, His very image, should subdue and have dominion over the earth and sea (Gen. 1:26–28).

Therefore fathers have the right and responsibility to be images of the King in their homes. Without denigrating the essential equality of their children as fellow human beings, they must exercise authority as one servant supervises another in the Master's household. First Timothy 3:4 tells us that one qualification of serving as an elder is to "rule well his own house, having his children in subjection with all gravity." Paul adds in verse 5, "For if a man know not how to rule his own house, how shall he take care of the church of God?" God wants us to follow this kingly concept as parents in the home.

We are to be teaching prophets as well as interceding and sacrificing priests. You can be friends with your children, but you are *more* than that; in the Lord, you are their authority figure. We are to be kings in the home whose rule is *just*, *wise*, and *loving*.

How does the head of a household exercise this loving authority? Here are two ways.

1. *Defend your children*. The king is the prime warrior of a kingdom. He leads his people into battle. So it was with Saul and David (1 Sam. 10:1; 2 Sam. 5:1–3; cf. 1 Sam. 18:13) and it is with Jesus Christ, the Divine Warrior (Rev. 19:11–16). Revelation 17:14 says, "These shall make war with the Lamb, and the Lamb shall overcome them: for he is Lord of lords, and King of kings: and they that are with him are called, and chosen, and faithful." The Bible says that every Christian is engaged in spiritual war against the devil and his forces (Eph. 6:10–20).

We have physical enemies who must be met with physical force, which God has authorized (Rom. 13:1–7). At times, a father must defend his family from physical danger. But I refer here to a father's responsibility to defend his family spiritually. We fight spiritual war with divine weapons, not weapons of the flesh (2 Cor. 10:4–5); fathers must fight this battle with the kingly authority entrusted to them to defend their precious ones.

For example, you should defend your children against the ungodly abuse of electronic media. Cell phones can receive and send pornography. Cults can recruit children through Internet chat rooms. We need a system to control the use of modern media in our homes. If we do not monitor and limit the use of these devices, our children may become passive observers, sitting for hours in front of the television, texting, e-mailing, or playing video games. Communications technology can be helpful, but it also creates an illusion of intimacy without fostering real relationships or an active life of service. Our goal as godly parents is not to raise couch potatoes. Your children may not appreciate the limitations you impose upon their use of such devices, but they will appreciate your taking time to provide family-oriented alternatives, such as reading to them, playing games and sports together, or involving them in your own work or recreational pursuits.

Also, defend your children against unwise romantic relationships. Romantic love can be stronger than death, and young people often lack the wisdom to discern the end results of immediate choices. In the United States dating is viewed as an activity for personal pleasure. The very idea of parental supervision may seem archaic and burdensome, but in Proverbs we see the wise father repeatedly warning his young son against immoral women (2:16–19; 5:1–23; 6:20–35; 7:1–27). The law of Moses recognized the father's authority over his daughter's commitments while she lived at home (Ex. 22:16–17; Num. 30:3–5). Human sexuality is both precious and dangerous. It should never be reduced to just casual entertainment. Sexuality is the glue that bonds a man and woman together for a lifetime and thus all families and society.

Fathers should be involved in regulating the relationships of their children with members of the opposite sex. You need not be an overprotective tyrant toward your children. I am not advocating a ban on all courting or "Christian dating." But reasonable rules and godly counsel in the context of a loving relationship with your children will go a long way to defend them against our sexually perverse culture. A young woman will feel protected knowing that a boy must speak to her father before dating her. A young man will feel more secure knowing that his parents will not leave him alone with a girl in the evening. Do we put dry straw next to fire and not expect it to burn? Develop good relationships with your children before they reach adolescence, and extend those relationships to their friends so they will value your counsel and respect your authority, even when their emotions go against your decisions.

Defend your children against unjust authorities. Are you willing to go to bat for your child if his schoolteacher or coach requires him to do something that violates his conscience? King Lemuel's mother told him, "Open thy mouth for the dumb in the cause of all such as are appointed to destruction. Open thy mouth, judge righteously, and plead the cause of the poor and needy" (Prov. 31:8–9). If that applies to kings and their subjects, how much more should fathers speak up for their children? I am not offering an excuse for public temper tantrums or political manipulation. But a father should stand up for his children against powerful and intimidating figures with fearless, respectful integrity. He must also teach them to stand up for themselves against such injustice.

Be a gentle warrior for your family. This will help them know that you have taken a clear stand on certain questions. They can then stand up to peer pressure by leaning on you. Do not weaken and try to be a passive, popular dad. That will force your children to stand alone against a wicked generation. Your children will love and respect you far more if you use your kingly authority to defend them from evil, but even if they do not, your exercising of kingly authority still brings glory to Christ.

2. *Discipline your children.* Jesus says in Revelation 3:19, "As many as I love, I rebuke and chasten [or discipline]: be zealous therefore, and repent." Christ is the perfect image of God the Father, of whom Hebrews 12:6 says, "For whom the Lord loveth he chasteneth, and scourgeth every son whom he receiveth." Therefore, it comes as no surprise that the Bible often calls fathers to discipline their children, even corporally (Prov. 13:24; 19:18; 22:15; 23:13–14; 29:15, 17; Eph. 6:4). Spanking has become a complex subject in our age of antiauthoritarianism, children's rights, and legitimate concerns about

abuse. While I cannot speak to every case, let me offer you some principles for discipline that reflect the kingship of Christ.

- Discipline your children in love. Before dealing with your child, search your heart. Are you disciplining your child in genuine love, mercy, and tenderness? Never discipline while your heart is full of wrath. Biblical discipline is always an act of love. Take a small child onto your lap; sit down next to an older one. Speak kindly in your admonitions. Your child will recognize kindness and will respond accordingly. Do not provoke your children to anger.

- Discipline your children only after instruction and reproof. Do not discipline a childish misunderstanding, only willful disobedience to a clear and specific command. Be careful here in discerning one from the other. For example, "Clean up your room," is far less clear to a child than, "Put all the toys that are on the floor back into the toy box." Make sure your child understands your expectations. Even then, you should ordinarily try a verbal rebuke before spanking a child.

- As needed, discipline your young children with appropriate use of corporal punishment. In the past, the liberal use of rods and canes was often abuse, so we must guard against that, but contrary to some opinions or even the laws of some countries, spanking is not physical abuse. The best Father in the universe says to us, "He that spareth his rod hateth his son: but he that loveth him chasteneth him betimes" (Prov. 13:24). If you never spank your young children, you are acting more out of self-love than in their best interests. A firm spank on a child's rear end will not injure him, but will teach him what mere words cannot: sin hurts. It is far better to learn that lesson with a spank than with a lifetime of disobedience culminating in eternal death.

- Discipline your children in honor. As you discipline your child, treat him as a human being created in the image of God. Discipline is best done in private unless a public sin requires a public rebuke. Never humiliate a child in front of others. Discipline is a form of honor in which you treat children as responsible, thinking people.

- Discipline your children with consistency, judgment, and self-control. Never act in anger or on impulse. Never exceed the bounds of what is necessary and safe. Never threaten a consequence unless you are committed to imposing it. Justice demands consistency. If you only discipline children when they push you to your emotional limits, then you are training them not in righteousness but in revenge. This is perhaps the most difficult requirement in discipline, since we all have times of fatigue or emotional weakness. Sometimes we might even find ourselves laughing in amusement at a child whom we need to discipline. Consistent discipline will

help your children see past you to the unchang-
ing law of God.

- Discipline your children for repentance. Always
  remember that the goal of discipline, as our Lord
  said, is that those we love should repent and be
  zealous for God. In other words, discipline aims
  at restoration of relationships, first between us
  and God, and second between us and other people. This keeps discipline within the bounds of
  love, for it is not for the sake of retributive justice
  to give deserved punishment, but for the sake of
  restorative mercy to win back those going astray.
  A spanking should be like the tap of the shep-
  herd's staff on the side of a sheep headed for the
  edge of a cliff.

- Discipline your children in prayerful humility.
  Do not discipline in an attempt to control your
  children. You will soon discover you cannot.
  Children have their own wills, and we are not
  God. Discipline is a form of human guidance.
  Therefore we must join our instructions, rebukes,
  appeals, and spankings to sincere petitions to the
  Lord that He will take away the heart of stone
  and give a heart of flesh to our children. He alone
  is the King of hearts.

### CONCLUSION

All fathers feel guilt (and they should) about their
failures and inadequacy in leading their families.
So let me offer a few words of encouragement to

you who are anointed to bear the threefold office of Christ in your home.

You may feel like a father who was once discouraged because things were not going well with his children. He did not know what to do. A friend saw what was happening and said, "Remember that the essence of parenting is to make disciples, and the One with all authority in heaven and on earth said, 'I am with you.'" So let me remind you, men, that if you become discouraged in trying to lead your family in discipleship, the Lord Christ says to you, "I am with you alway, even unto the end of the world" (Matt. 28:20).

We cannot exercise the offices of Christ apart from Christ. Apart from Him you can do nothing, but if you abide in Him you will bear much fruit. Look to Him. Rely upon His Holy Spirit, who anoints you out of His fullness. When guilt and shame threaten you, take your sins as a husband and father to your Great High Priest. Wash your conscience in His precious blood. Cry out to the Lamb who was slain so that you can love your wife and children as Christ loves His own. When you wonder if your prayers go further than the ceiling, remember that He who prays for you is seated on the right hand of God. Even as you exercise kingly authority to defend and discipline your children, be much in prayer to the King of kings, that He would conquer Satan and make your children willing to serve Him. Your weakness can become the platform where His strength is displayed so that your family will learn by watching you pray, "Thy grace is sufficient for us."

Faith in our "chief Prophet, only High Priest, and eternal King" will not make you passive, but confidently active. Therefore, in His name, use every opportunity to lead your family. Teach them. Love them. Sacrifice for them. Evangelize them. Pray for them. Rule them. Protect them. Persevere in faithfulness as a husband and father.

Perhaps you have failed to lead your children in the way of godliness. Perhaps you have been passive. Perhaps you have been abusive. Perhaps you see in yourself more of the image of the devil than the image of our Prophet, Priest, and King. You have fallen short of providing leadership in your home. It is never too late to start evangelizing your children or to speak to them about spiritual things. It is never too late to confess your own sin to them, even after they have moved out of the home. It is never too late for you to find grace and mercy from the great Prophet, Priest, and King. Perhaps God will grant you the opportunity to help your children by instructing your grandchildren in the ways of God. Use every opportunity you are given to influence the grandchildren God has given to you. Let me close with the prayer of a seventeenth-century Puritan:

> Let those that are united to me in tender ties be precious in Thy sight, and devoted to Thy glory. Sanctify and prosper my domestic devotion, my domestic instruction, my domestic discipline,

my domestic example, that my house may be a nursery for heaven and a church as the garden of the Lord, enriched as trees of righteousness of Thy planting for Thy glory. Let not those in my family fall short of heaven at last, but grant that the promising appearances of tender consciences, of soft hearts, of the alarms and delights of Thy Word may not be blotted out, but may bring forth judgment unto victory in all those whom I love.